Teddy and The Gipper:

A Notre Dame Friendship

By

Len Clark, Ph.D.

ISBN: 979-8-35096-656-5 (Paperback)

Library of Congress Control Number: 2024912108

Any references to historical events, real people, or real places are used factitiously. Names, characters, and places are products of the author's imagination.

Front and back cover images by Jared Basker

Printed by Book Baby in the United States of America.

First printing edition 2024.

LTC Media, LLC
5303 Central Ave.
Portage, IN 46368

www.teddyandthegipper.com

This book is a fantastic read for any student and athlete, emphasizing the importance of striving for greatness in all endeavors. It resonates deeply with the values we teach at Portage High School—leadership, perseverance, and teamwork. As the Athletic Director, I find the connection between our high school and Notre Dame, a symbol of excellence nearby, truly inspiring."

*Brett St. Germaine*
*Athletic Director, Portage High School*


"A timeless story of what it means to fall in love with a place and to keep to it in your heart for a lifetime. The Spirit of Notre Dame sparks in Teddy and Snacks right away as they explore the campus and take in its beautiful architecture, and as they bond with unforgettable figures like Knute Rockne and George Gipp. Their story invites the reader to fall in love, or perhaps re-fall in love, with the university and its historical connections to the nearby communities in Northern Indiana."

*Austin Bonta*
*Mayor of Portage, Indiana*


"Teddy and the Gipper" beautifully captures the enduring spirit and camaraderie that define Notre Dame. My friend Len Clark brings to life a friendship that embodies many of Notre Dame's greatest values and symbolizes the university's mission which traces back to Fr. Sorin's prediction of becoming a "great force for good in the world."   A must-read for those looking to understand what makes Notre Dame unique, with some football tossed in."

*Cappy Gagnon, ND' 66*


"I spent my adult life around Notre Dame and was blessed to get four decades as the PA announcer at the Stadium. Yet, I think Len has me beat, at least a little. But he, like me, is always fair in his judgements. And he is not an Honorary USC Trojans like me. They honored me when I retired, and I am proud of it."

*Mike Collins*
*Former Notre Dame Stadium Public Address Announcer*

Teddy and The Gipper: A Notre Dame Friendship

By

Len Clark, Ph.D.

LTC Media Publishing

PORTAGE, IN - DUBLIN, IRELAND

# *Dedication*

This book is dedicated to the enduring spirits of Notre Dame—
*Past, Present, and Future.*

To the dreamers, believers, and storytellers who find a piece of
themselves within its storied walls, *Teddy and The Gipper: A
Notre Dame Friendship* celebrates the unbreakable bonds of
camaraderie, the timeless tradition of excellence, and the shared
journeys that connect us all.

It is a tribute to those who dare to dream and those who believe
in the magic of this storied institution.

May the tales of Teddy, Snacks, the Gipper, and the countless
others who have walked these hallowed grounds inspire you to
cherish your connections, pursue your passions with zeal, and
uphold the spirit of the Fighting Irish with pride.

This narrative is more than a recounting of historical moments;
it's a beacon for those who seek inspiration and a testament to
the power of enduring friendships and shared destinies.

Here's to the friendships that light our way, the dreams that
propel us forward, and the indomitable Fighting Irish spirit that
dwells within each of us.

May these stories also enrich your life and remind you of the
shared humanity that binds us together.

Welcome to our story, where Notre Dame legends come alive,
and the legacy of the Fighting Irish continues to inspire
generation after generation.

# Acknowledgments

I am immensely thankful to those who inspired me on this journey, with special recognition to my family, especially my mother, Gloria Clark. Thank you for helping me chase my dreams. And to the following individuals:

Dervilla Flynn, for just about everything, and for making the Dublin project a reality. You are my best friend.

Jim *'Augie'* Augustine, of Augie's Locker Room, for your friendship and support of my Notre Dame projects.

Ron, Cheri, Danny, RJ, Nick, Tommy, Pat, Christine, George, *'The Gas Man,'* Tom, Skip, *'The Big Sexy',* you make game days special.

Bob Lovell, host of *Indiana Sport Talk,* thank you for the opportunity to update listeners across Indiana about Notre Dame athletics on your show.

My teachers at Central Elementary, Aylesworth Junior High, and Portage High School, in Portage, Indiana, for your encouragement and guidance.

My friend, Tony Roberts, forever known as the *'Voice of Notre Dame Football.'* I miss your dulcet tones and our enjoyable conversations.

John Miley of *The Miley Collection* , for your friendship and introducing me to your collection.

Jack Freeman, in today's AI age, I wonder what projects we could have done together.

And to the students I have taught and worked with at Indiana State University, Kentucky Wesleyan College, the University of Evansville, Virginia Tech, Michigan State University, the Irish Academy of Public Relations, and the University of Notre Dame - thank you for being part of my journey.

# *Preface*

Notre Dame has been a foundational pillar in my life, a sentiment that many of you also share, especially those who grew up watching its football highlights, brought to life by the legendary broadcasting duo of Lindsey Nelson and Paul Hornung, on Sunday mornings.

My childhood was profoundly shaped by Notre Dame, from the countless times I borrowed *Knute Rockne: Young Athlete* from the Central Elementary School Library in Portage, Indiana, to the impact that meeting Coach Ara Parseghian had on me.

Attending my first Notre Dame football game in 1972—and witnessing a dramatic loss to Missouri in the rain—left an indelible mark on me. Decades later as a broadcast journalist, my lifelong passion inspired me to create an audio package, which aired on the Notre Dame Radio Network, on the storied rivalry between Notre Dame and USC, which earned me the national *Powerade Award* from the National Sports Media Association.

My journey also led me to teach in the university's *Gallivan Journalism Program*, where I worked with the next generation of journalists while continuing to cover Notre Dame athletics using emerging media technologies.

The inspiration for *Teddy and the Gipper: A Notre Dame Friendship* stems from my deep appreciation for Indiana history, my hometown of Portage, Indiana, and the rich narratives associated with Notre Dame. Collaborating with fans and covering the *'Fighting Irish'* has only deepened my connection to this storied institution.

I'm delighted to present this historical fiction tribute to our collective Notre Dame spirit.

Len Clark, Ph.D.
Portage, Indiana
March 15, 2024

# Chapter One

## Mr. Ted Flynn

Theodore Liam Flynn, Jr., known as 'Ted,' to his friends and 'Mr. Flynn' by his students, had just finished teaching his final term at Portage High School, ending a 40+ year career that began as a student-teacher at South Bend Central High School.

During his tenure at the school in Northwest Indiana, he taught social studies and government, served as dean of students, and was a member of the football coaching staff when Portage started a program in the early 1950s.

Since classes had concluded earlier that week, his plan that Friday morning was to finish grading papers in his classroom, where he had been teaching since the 'new' high school opened its doors for the 1954-1955 school year. He also aimed to collect his personal belongings and to get the room ready for the new teacher.

*The third and current Portage High School opened for the 1979-1980 school year. The former high school is now Willowcreek Middle School.*

As he glanced down to begin grading essays on 'Foundations of the U.S. Government,' his thoughts drifted back to 1933, the year he started teaching at Portage High School as a young man.

A knock on his classroom door suddenly snapped him out of his daydream.

"Hi, Mr. Flynn, it's me, Patty. Here are the boxes you asked for."

"Thank you, Patty," Ted said. "Just put them on a desk in the back of the room, please."

Ambitious Patty Greenway had just completed her junior year and was looking forward to becoming a senior in the fall, proudly representing the *PHS Class of 1974.*

She was helping at the high school that morning by running errands and doing small tasks for teachers and administrators.

"We're sure going to miss you next year, Mr. Flynn," said Patty.

She then added, "Principal Smith told me to ask you if there's anything you need or if I can help you in any way."

"As a matter of fact, you can," said Ted. "I have a few items remaining on the back shelf that need to be boxed, and I would greatly appreciate your help."

Patty grabbed one of the cardboard boxes and walked to the back shelf, where she began placing items neatly into the large brown box.

The items on the shelf spanned the decades and told stories of Ted's teaching career and past.

She examined each item one by one, carefully, as if she were a museum curator, before gently placing it into Ted's *'box of memories.'*

The items included yearbooks, coffee mugs, books, Notre Dame memorabilia, and a Portage Basketball 1972 Sectional Champions T-shirt.

A few of his treasures, though, caught her eye and made her curious.

One was a picture in a faded wooden frame of a boy and his dog, which had been in Ted's classroom since his first day as a teacher.

Another item was an old-fashioned, autographed football, the writing on which was so faint that she had to squint to make it out.

14

And then, there was a picture of Ted with Coach Larry Casbon alongside Tom Reynolds, a 1965 Portage High School graduate, and a member of the 1966 Notre Dame national championship football team.

"Mr. Flynn," Patty said, "you must really be a huge Notre Dame fan."

"I am," Ted replied. "Class of '32."

"I like the Fighting Irish, too," she said. "My dad and I never miss a game on TV, and we watch the replay highlights religiously on Sunday mornings with Lindsey Nelson and Paul Hornung.

Patty then asked, "I know you're busy grading papers, but could you tell me about a few of these items when you have time?"

"Sure," Ted said, as he looked up from his grading. "What would you like to know?"

"Well, I know the person in this picture with you and Coach Casbon is Tom Reynolds," she said.

"Tom was in my sister Gloria's class, but who is the boy in this picture with the dog? And where did you get this autographed football?" Patty added.

"I remember Gloria," Ted said with a smile, as he rose from his desk and walked towards the back shelf where Patty was working.

"She and Tom were good students," he added.

"Tom's working on his Ph.D. in mathematical psychology at USC," said Ted, beaming with pride. "And he always stops by to see me when he's back in town. How's your sister doing?" Ted asked.

"She's doing great," said Patty. "Thank you for asking. She studied nursing at the University of Evansville and is now a pediatric nurse living in Indianapolis."

"I'm glad to hear that," Ted said. "Gloria always talked about becoming a nurse."

Ted looked into the large brown cardboard box and then reached in to pick up the framed picture of the boy and the dog.

He began to smile as he stared into the picture from his past, as his mind drifted back to a simpler time when he was known as 'Teddy' and to the day he received the football.

"Patty, this is a picture of me as a young boy," he said. "I haven't looked at it in a very long time."

Feeling a bit nostalgic, Ted then said to Patty, "I think I need to take a break from grading for a while."

"Should I leave?" Asked Patty.

"No, please stay," Ted said. He then added, "Patty, how would you like to hear the story about the day I got this football and made a friend?"

"Really, are you sure?" asked Patty.

"I'm sure and my grading can wait," Ted said, as the two sat down. "Plus, I always have time to talk about Notre Dame."

Eager to catch every word, Patty leaned forward, while Ted placed the picture of the boy and the dog in front of him.

He then retrieved the weathered football from the box and placed it in front of Patty.

Ted looked at the two items for a moment, as memories of days gone by poured back to him, as he gathered his thoughts.

After a moment of reflection, Ted nodded his head and smiled as he started to tell Patty the story from his childhood.

Now, if you have a moment, and are interested in learning about how Teddy got that autographed football and made a friend, I'd like to share that story with you.

# Chapter Two

## Saying Goodbye to Chicago

Teddy didn't want to move.

He dreaded the thought of leaving everything he had always known behind.

Plus, he liked Chicago, and had many friends in his little neighborhood on the city's South Side and was well-liked by his classmates and teacher.

Teddy was in the third grade, played second base for the neighborhood baseball team, and served as an altar boy on Sundays at St. Patrick Catholic Church.

The Flynn family, like many first-generation Irish-Catholic families, embraced their new life in America, and Teddy truly embodied the spirit of an *All-American* boy back in 1919.

But things were about to dramatically change for him and his family.

You see, Teddy's dad was offered a job at the Studebaker plant in his hometown of South Bend, Indiana, where he would lead a team of skilled auto workers to assemble a new six-cylinder engine car model that was being produced.

It was a well-paying job, too, so Teddy's mom and dad decided it was best for their family to move back to South Bend.

*Studebaker, at that time, was one of the biggest auto manufacturers in the United States. The company began by building wagons in the city in 1852, and then started making automobiles in 1902.*

*In fact, Studebaker was one of the first car manufacturers to produce an electric vehicle, the 'Studebaker Electric,' a battery-powered car, that was sold from 1902 to 1912. It also produced the 'Rockne' from 1932 to 1933 at its plant in Detroit, Michigan. Sadly, the Studebaker Corporation closed its South Bend plant in 1963.*

*Today, however, The Studebaker National Museum in South Bend showcases a variety of its automobiles, wagons, carriages, and military vehicles, and hosts international gatherings for enthusiasts.*

So, until the Flynn family found a new home, they were going to stay with Teddy's paternal grandparents, Mary Catherine (O'Shea) Flynn, his *'Gran,'* and William Theodore Flynn, his *'Grandad.'*

Now, South Bend was only 100 miles or so away from Teddy's home in Chicago, but to him it might as well have been a thousand as he didn't want to move and leave his school, teacher, and especially his best friend, *'Jimmy'* behind.

Teddy understood how important this new job was for his family, but he was still sad about the impending move and the upcoming changes.

It was hard on him, as it would be for any nine-year-old boy.

That Thursday morning was just another typical April day in Chicago for Teddy.

He got up at seven o'clock in the morning, got dressed, ate his breakfast, and then hurried out the front door to meet Jimmy.

"Jimmy, I sure hope you find someone to play second base after I move," said Teddy, as they walked along the sidewalk to school.

It would be their last walk together to Central Elementary School as Teddy and his family were moving to South Bend the very next day.

After a day of the 'Three Rs' - *Reading, wRiting, and aRithmetic,* Teddy's teacher, Mrs. Snyder, told the class that Teddy was moving and would not be coming back to school.

As his class got ready to leave, Teddy's friends wished him well and gave him a few pats on the back for good luck as he headed home with his best friend by his side for one final time.

Mrs. Snyder also wished Teddy well and told him to do his best at his new school. She then gave him a little gift with a card that said:

*"Remember, Teddy, every challenge is an opportunity in disguise. You have the strength and courage to face anything that comes your way. Believe in yourself as much as we all believe in you - Mrs. Snyder."*

There was still about a month of school left before summer vacation, so Teddy would have to attend a new school in South Bend.

The thought of a new school and living in a new city was quite frightening to him, but at least he had *'Snacks,'* his dog, to be with him.

Snacks was a lovable, loyal, floppy-eared ragamuffin and the epitome of an *All-American* mutt.

But to Teddy, Snacks meant the world, and the two of them were like *'two peas in a pod'* and did everything together.

Early that Friday morning, Teddy, Snacks, and Teddy's mom and dad loaded up their Studebaker for the move.

As the last box was loaded into the car, a sense of both excitement and apprehension filled the air, marking the beginning of a new chapter in their lives.

As the car slowly pulled away from the curb, Jimmy waved a final farewell as he began to walk to school by himself for the first time without Teddy.

"Come see me in South Bend!" shouted Teddy, as the car headed east towards the *'Hoosier State.'*

Jimmy continued to wave goodbye until the Flynn family car slowly disappeared from his sight.

# Chapter Three

# Off to South Bend

The trip to South Bend would take only a few hours, and along the way, they would pass by the steel mills in Gary, Indiana, and then through Portage Township, the area Teddy would eventually call home for many years.

They traveled along the Indiana coastline of Lake Michigan on what was known as the old *'Detroit-Chicago Pike.'*

*The Detroit-Chicago Pike was a military road constructed along the former Great Sauk Indian Trail, that linked Detroit with Fort Dearborn (Chicago). The two-lane highway was later designated as the 'Dunes Highway' or U.S. 12 in 1926, and is now part of the Lake Michigan Circle Tour, a designated scenic road system that connects the Great Lakes and the St. Lawrence River.*

It was a beautiful day to travel.

A little over an hour into the trip, they decided to stop for a break in Michigan City, Indiana, where they would have a picnic lunch at Washington Park.

*Michigan City is the hometown of Notre Dame President, Father Robert Dowd, C.S.C., as well as actress Anne Baxter, baseball player Don Larsen, and Medal of Honor recipient Daniel Bruce. Today, many of Notre Dame's football opponents stay at the Blue Chip Casino Hotel Spa in the city.*

There, they ate the ham sandwiches and boiled eggs Teddy's mom had packed for the trip and drank lemonade on the beach near the pier that leads out to the lighthouse overlooking Lake Michigan.

*Built in 1904, the lighthouse has become the most popular symbol of Michigan City and is the only public operating lighthouse in Indiana.*

As Teddy and his family enjoyed their lunch, Snacks barked and chased the seagulls who hovered over them begging for morsels of food.

"You have to be faster than that to catch one," laughed Teddy, as Snacks continued to jump and play with the fearless scavengers.

After lunch, Teddy helped his mom fold the family picnic blanket and ensured all the sand was removed from his shoes. Then, he climbed back into the Studebaker for the final leg of their trip to South Bend.

"Another hour or so, and we'll be at Grandma Flynn's house," said Teddy's dad as they drove down the road that would eventually become U.S. 20 before turning onto the Lincoln Highway.

*U.S. 20 is an east-west highway that stretches across the entire United States from New England to the Pacific Northwest, and is now, officially, recognized as the 'National Medal of Honor Highway.'*

*The Lincoln Highway, one of the first transcontinental highways in the United States, was one of the first highways designed expressly for automobiles. In Indiana, the original route went through South Bend and Elkhart. The historic route, which opened in 1913, stretches from New York to San Francisco and spans 14 states and 700 cities, towns, and villages.*

As they navigated the often-unpaved roads meandering through the northern Indiana countryside, which featured open fields - a stark contrast to the bustling industrial landscapes of Chicago that Teddy was accustomed to - they passed through the towns of Rolling Prairie and New Carlisle.

Teddy looked out of the window of the Studebaker, fascinated by the scenery, while Snacks stuck his head out of the other window, with his tongue hanging out and flapping in the breeze.

"When was the last time I was at Grandma Flynn's house?" Teddy asked his mother.

"We haven't been back home since you were a wee baby," she said. "I know the move has been hard on you, but please keep an open mind, Teddy."

"I will, Mom," Teddy said. "I promise."

Later that afternoon, the Flynn family's Studebaker finally rolled into the gravel driveway of Teddy's grandmother's house.

As they climbed out of the car, Snacks eagerly bounded ahead, his tail wagging with excitement. The scent of freshly cut grass and blooming flowers filled the air, marking a refreshing end to the long journey they had just completed.

Teddy then followed, taking in the vibrant views and cozy charm of his grandmother's house. It was a moment of hope and anticipation, marking the start of their new life in South Bend, filled with adventures and memories waiting to be made.

# Chapter Four

## Grandma Flynn

Grandma Flynn's story is typical of many immigrants to America.

She, her husband William, and their baby Teddy (Teddy's dad) left their home in Ireland with not much more than hope and a prayer and made their way to America.

Back in Ireland, they had heard stories about America as the land of opportunities, and she was determined to find a better future for her family.

So, the young family saved their money, bought passage on a ship, crossed the Atlantic Ocean, and eventually settled in South Bend, Indiana, drawn by its job opportunities and a growing Irish community.

Their journey wasn't just about moving from one country to another; it was about laying the groundwork for their family's future, all while keeping their Irish spirit alive and kicking.

Grandma Flynn lived in a yellow, postage-stamp-sized house with a big oak tree in the front yard. She was sitting on the front porch swing, waiting for Teddy, his mom and dad, and Snacks to arrive.

Teddy's grandfather, *'Grandad'*, worked for the South Bend Branch of the Pennsylvania Railroad and was away in Logansport, Indiana, working on a project. However, he would be back home by the end of the week.

"Hello, hello, everyone! How are we?" Grandma Flynn exclaimed excitedly as she rushed down the porch stairs to embrace everyone and to hug and kiss Teddy.

Snacks, clearly delighted to see her, received a gentle pat on the head.

After unpacking the car and telling Grandma Flynn about their trip, Teddy and his family began to settle in for the evening and prepare for dinner.

Grandma Flynn was a good cook and had made her specialty, chicken & noodles, that evening, plus her famous Irish apple tart for dessert to mark the special occasion.

She even had a large bone for Snacks.

Teddy's dad started the meal by saying grace: *'Bless us, O Lord, and these, Thy gifts, which we are about to receive from Thy bounty, through Christ, our Lord.'*

"Amen!" Teddy said. "Moving sure made me hungry," he added, as Snacks chewed on his bone underneath the kitchen table.

"Eat up, everybody," Grandma Flynn said. "There's plenty for everyone."

After finishing dinner, Teddy helped with the dishes and told Grandma Flynn about what he was learning in school, playing baseball and, of course, his best friend Jimmy.

As Teddy dried and put away the last dish, he began to yawn.

After wishing everyone goodnight, he slowly climbed the stairs with Snacks by his side, leading to the room that would be his for the next few months, to go to bed.

It had been a long day for him, and as soon as he said his prayers and his head hit the pillow, he fell fast asleep with Snacks curled up by the foot of his bed.

That night, Teddy found himself immersed in an incredibly vivid dream, unlike anything he could have ever imagined, as he slept.

It was like the dream was telling him about a journey he was going to take, packed with many tough challenges and amazing accomplishments.

In the dream he saw himself in a classroom, excitedly talking to students, facing tough challenges that really tested his grit, and celebrating wins that made him feel proud.

As the dream unfolded, Teddy felt a profound sense of purpose and determination, as if the universe was offering him a glimpse into the incredible journey that awaited him.

Beside him, Snacks wagged his tail energetically, as if sensing the excitement and sharing in the anticipation of the adventures they would embark on together.

# Chapter Five

## Saturday Morning

Teddy awoke that Saturday morning to the wonderful aroma of breakfast cooking and sleepily walked down the stairs to the kitchen, rubbing the sleep from his eyes.

There, near the stove, was Grandma Flynn wearing a bright red apron tied around her waist, singing a traditional Irish song, and cooking Teddy's favorite breakfast - scrambled eggs and bacon.

Teddy's father had already left for the day for a meeting at the Studebaker plant, and his mother was out doing errands.

So, it was just Grandma Flynn, Teddy, and Snacks.

Grandma Flynn heard footsteps and turned around to see the two coming down the stairs.

She then said, in an Irish brogue, "Good morning, Teddy. How did you sleep? Are you hungry? How's my boy?"

Grandma Flynn then said, "and good morning to you, too, Snacks. How is the *'King of the Castle'* this morning?"

Now, Teddy's grandmother was from County Mayo in Ireland, but despite being in the United States for nearly 30 years, she still had a strong Irish accent.

*County Mayo is also the boyhood home of Notre Dame graduate and 'Rosary Priest' Father Patrick Peyton, C.S.C.*

"Fine, Gran," said Teddy, as he sat down to eat his breakfast while Snacks was underneath the kitchen table chewing on his bone.

"Gran?" said Teddy, "I miss my friend Jimmy and Chicago."

"I know you do," Grandma Flynn said, as she sat down at the table with Teddy and took a sip of her tea. "I know just how you feel."

"You do?" Teddy questioned.

"I do," Grandma Flynn said with conviction. "When we left Ireland for America it was a sad day for us, too, as we had to leave our family and friends."

"But do you know what?" Grandma Flynn said with passion in her voice. "It was also an exciting time for us because it was an adventure, and we knew it was the right decision."

*During the 1800s, over 5 million people emigrated from Ireland to the United States due to religious conflicts, lack of political autonomy, and the 'Great Famine.'*

"It was?" said Teddy.

"It sure was," she said. "You'll make new friends, Teddy. I know you will. It'll just take a little time," she added, with a wink and a smile.

Grandma Flynn also told Teddy to write a letter to Jimmy and invite him to come to South Bend over the summer vacation.

"He can take the South Shore and before you know it, he'll be here in South Bend," she added.

*The South Shore is a train line that runs from Chicago to South Bend, Indiana, and is one of the last interurban trains in the United States. It was built between 1901 and 1908 and continues to run to this day.*

You might have even taken the train to visit Chicago or the Indiana Dunes.

## Chapter Six

## 'Let's Go Exploring'

Teddy felt a little bit better knowing that Jimmy would be coming for a visit during the summer, but he still missed his best friend.

Grandma Flynn then suggested to Teddy that after breakfast that he and Snacks go on an adventure of their own and explore the neighborhood.

"Make sure you visit Notre Dame," she said, as the campus was only a few football fields away from her home.

It was a beautiful morning to go exploring for the two adventurers, with birds chirping and people working in their yards.

So, after breakfast, Teddy put on his cap, tied his shoes, and took a deep breath as he and Snacks headed out the door and down the porch to set off on their big adventure.

"Come on, boy," said Teddy. "Let's go exploring."

The two walked through Grandma Flynn's neighborhood, greeted the neighbors, explored the woods, and soon came upon the east side of the Notre Dame campus.

*The University of Notre Dame was founded in 1842 by Father Edward Sorin of the Congregation of Holy Cross (C.S.C.). It is a preeminent research university that offers an outstanding undergraduate and graduate education guided by a Catholic mission. Located in Notre Dame, Indiana it is adjacent to the city of South Bend and approximately 90 miles east of Chicago.*

As the two explorers got closer to campus, they could hear whistles and people yelling, so they went to investigate the area where the sound was coming from.

Soon they came upon a field where they saw football players practicing.

Some of the players were kicking and throwing footballs, while others were practicing their tackling drills.

It was the Notre Dame football team, and it was spring practice!

Teddy liked football.

He and Jimmy would play with their friends in the sandlot near his home in Chicago, and he knew all about Notre Dame from listening to the stories his dad told him about the famous football team and coach.

He also pretended to play for the 'Ramblers' and dreamed of one day scoring the winning touchdown for Notre Dame against Army.

*I know what you are thinking: Notre Dame is known as the 'Fighting Irish,' and you are correct. However, it wasn't until 1927 when the University and President Father Matthew Walsh officially adopted the nickname.*

As Teddy and Snacks got closer, they looked toward the north end of the football field and saw a majestic sight: the Golden Dome of the Notre Dame Administration Building gleaming in the April sun.

Teddy just stood there in awe of the spectacle. "What is this magical place?" he said.

Snacks just looked up at Teddy quizzically, with his head turned sideways.

Together, they were about to embark on the greatest adventure of their lives, at a place where their dreams would become reality.

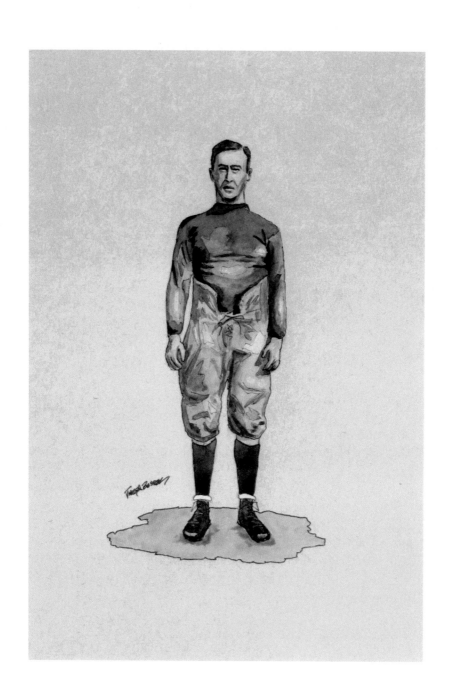

# Chapter Seven

## The Tall Football Player

Just about that time, a wayward football came bouncing towards them.

Snacks went up to sniff and investigate the strange object, as a tall, athletic-looking player came running over and said, "Hey, you, throw me the ball!"

Teddy went over to get the football, but Snacks had other plans and grabbed the football's laces with his teeth and briskly walked away with it.

The tall football player then yelled, "Come back with that football!"

But Snacks had no intention of giving the leather ball back to him, and proudly started playing with his new possession.

Teddy told the tall football player that he would get the ball back and said, "Gimme the ball, Snacks. Come on, boy, give it to me," while cautiously approaching the 'canine crook.'

Snacks, however, had other ideas and started to run away with the ball. Teddy chased after Snacks, yelling, and pleading for him to come back.

But Snacks, wanting to have some fun, ignored him, and continued to strut around the practice field as though he scored the game's winning touchdown.

The tall football player joined in the chase, as Snacks zig-zagged his way around the field and darted away from the two chasing him.

Snacks ran the two of them around in circles and every time they got too close to him, he would make a fake one way and then run in the opposite direction.

His antics even caught the attention of the Notre Dame football coach, who watched with keen interest.

"Hey, look at that little dog run," one football player yelled, as the practice suddenly came to a halt to watch Snacks.

The next thing you know the entire first-team defense joined in the chase, with Teddy yelling and crying for Snacks to stop.

He was afraid Snacks would get them into trouble, and he didn't know what to do if that happened.

"Snacks, please stop!" cried Teddy.

The chase continued for a few minutes, and the yelling for Snacks to stop suddenly turned into laughter, as the little dog cut to the left, zipped up the sideline with the football, and headed toward the end zone with the view of the Golden Dome.

The football coach even started to laugh and said, "Gipp, that's how you run with a football and avoid a defense. Take notes, boy! Do that and you'll make All-American."

Now, that coach knew a thing or two about dogs and football, and he knew the only way to get it back was to trick Snacks.

"Get me another pigskin, Kiley, and I'll show you how to stop a fullback," said the confident coach.

He whistled to catch Snacks' attention, and then held up a new football for the little dog to see.

Snacks stopped running and, with his ears perked up, looked over at the animated coach who was waving the football.

Snacks, with his tail wagging excitedly, walked over to the coach and dropped the ball at his feet.

He then barked at the balding man, dressed in a gray Notre Dame sweatshirt with a whistle around his neck, urging him to throw him the new ball.

While Snacks was distracted, the tall football player known as 'Gipp' snuck up from behind the little 'prankster pup' and snatched the football back.

"Got it!" yelled Gipp, as he dropped to the ground gasping for air while trying to catch his breath from all the running.

Between breaths he said to Teddy, "Your dog sure is fast."

"I know," Teddy panted. "Are we in trouble?"

"Trouble? Why, of course not," the tall football player said.

"We're not?" Questioned Teddy.

"No, you're not in trouble because you and your dog just gave me and the rest of the team the best workout we've had this spring!" Said the tall football player.

"Whew," Teddy sighed. "I thought we were in trouble for sure."

The tall football player laughed and said, "Kid, the only time people get into trouble around here is if they don't work hard in practice or hit the books studying."

Admitting defeat and having been outsmarted by the intelligent coach, Snacks returned to Teddy's side without a football.

Teddy then said, "Good news, boy. We're not in trouble!"

Snacks barked a sigh of relief.

# Chapter Eight

## Meeting Gipp and Coach Rockne

"I'm George Gipp," the tall football player said, as he stuck his hand out to shake Teddy's.

"I'm Teddy, Teddy Flynn, and this is my dog Snacks," he said as he felt the powerful grip of the tall football player's hand.

"Nice to meet you, Teddy," said Gipp. "You, too, Snacks," as he patted the little dog on the head.

"Ruff," Snacks barked as he stuck out his paw to say "hello."

"Say, I haven't seen you two around here before," Gipp said.

"We just moved here yesterday from Chicago and we're staying with my Grandma Flynn," said Teddy, as he sadly looked down toward the ground."

"Well, we're going to have to do something about that and welcome you to the neighborhood and Notre Dame," Gipp said.

"If you can wait for practice to get over, I'll buy you a root beer and show you and Snacks around campus," he added.

"Really?" beamed Teddy. "That'll be swell." Teddy then asked about the man with the whistle.

"Why, that's Coach Rockne," said Gipp. "He's the best coach in college football."

"Coach Rockne. That's Knute Rockne!" said Teddy with excitement.

Now, Teddy knew all about Coach Rockne from the stories his dad told him about how he helped Notre Dame beat Army in 1913 using the forward pass.

"Is that really him?" Teddy asked.

Gipp assured him that it was and said, "Come on, I'll introduce you and Snacks to him."

So, Teddy and Snacks met Coach Rockne, who invited them to watch practice from the sideline as the team went through their drills.

The charismatic football coach shouted out instructions and gave demonstrations during the practice, while Snacks, acting like the coach, barked out plays and chased loose footballs.

After the last whistle of practice was blown, each player came over to meet Snacks and to introduce themselves to Teddy.

Coach Rockne then walked over to give Snacks a scratch behind the ear.

He then said, "Teddy, Snacks gave me an idea for a running play that we're going to use this coming season against Kalamazoo, and for helping us out and giving me the idea, I'd like to give you this football."

*Notre Dame opened the 1919 football season at home at Cartier Field, where they defeated the Kalamazoo College Hornets 14-0. The first points of the season were set up by a long run by George Gipp.*

"A football for me? Really, for keeps?" Teddy said. "Gee, thanks, wait until Jimmy sees this!"

"You're welcome, sport," said Coach Rockne. "I'd also like to invite you and Snacks to be my guests at the opening game."

"Gee whiz!" said Teddy with excitement. "I've never been to a football game before. Thank you, Mr. Rockne."

*Commemorate your first Notre Dame game by purchasing a Notre Dame Football Heritage Project certificate at www.ndcertificate.com*

"Call me *Rock*," he said. "You and Snacks can stop by practice anytime you're in the neighborhood and be our mascots."

38

He then turned away and walked towards the Golden Dome.

Now, Notre Dame has had a history of canine mascots dating back to 1909, when a picture of the 1909 Western Champion Notre Dame football team featured an American Bulldog named *'Mike.'*

*In 1924, the Notre Dame Alumni Club of Toledo presented Coach Rockne with an Irish Terrier named 'Tipperary Terrence', who began a line of Irish Terrier mascots for the Notre Dame football team.*

*The Irish Terriers included 'Brick Top Shaun Rhu', from 1932 to 1933, and 'Clashmore Mike', who took over in the 1935 season.*

*'Clashmore Mike' would cheer for Fighting Irish football teams until the 1960s, when the Leprechaun logo, created by artist Ted Drake, made its debut as a mascot in 1964.*

Teddy looked down at his *'canine companion'* and said, "Gee, Snacks, this day sure has turned out to be a great adventure. I can't wait to tell everyone and show them our new football!"

Upon hearing this, Gipp asked Jack Freeman, the head equipment manager, for a pen and said, "Teddy, I'm even going to sign that football for you."

Gipp then wrote on the football, "To Teddy and Snacks from your friend, George Gipp."

Teddy and Snacks looked at each other in awe, realizing that this simple gesture connected them to the storied legacy of Notre Dame, making them feel truly part of something special and timeless.

## Chapter Nine

## Getting To Know Notre Dame & South Bend

After practice and as the sun beamed down over the Notre Dame campus, Teddy, Snacks, and George Gipp strolled through the picturesque grounds of the university.

Gipp pointed out the iconic campus landmarks, which included Sacred Heart Parish, the Grotto of Our Lady of Lourdes, and Washington Hall.

*Sacred Heart Parish was elevated to the rank of Minor Basilica on January 17, 1992, and is now known as the Basilica of the Sacred Heart.*

"You know, Teddy, Notre Dame is more than just football," Gipp said. "It's a community and a family. You'll find friends here, just like you did in Chicago," he added.

He then said, "and, if you study really hard, you, too, might have a chance to go to school here in a couple of years."

Teddy felt warmth in his heart as he listened to Gipp's words while enjoying his ice-cold root beer. Snacks also had a refreshment by lapping water from a hose at the Notre Dame Science Hall.

*The Notre Dame Science Hall opened in 1883, and later became the LaFortune Student Center, or 'The Huddle', in 1953.*

Teddy then began to realize that maybe South Bend wouldn't be so bad after all, with a newfound friend in George Gipp and the support of Snacks, things were starting to look up for him.

Over the next few days, Teddy and Snacks explored more of their new neighborhood and South Bend.

They visited Howard Park, where they met some local kids playing baseball who invited them to join in their game.

A few of them, around his age, became good pals with Teddy. They included Mike *'Pee Wee'* Warner, Eddy *'Ned'* Dawson, and Jim *'Lure King'* Houk, who also shared a passion for sports and Notre Dame.

Snacks, always the center of attention, became the group's unofficial mascot and star left fielder.

Grandma Flynn also encouraged Teddy to participate in activities at his new school, St. Joseph Elementary, believing it would help him make even more friends.

And she was right.

A few weeks later, on another beautiful sunny afternoon in South Bend, Teddy and Snacks and their new friends were playing baseball in the vacant lot across from Grandma Flynn's house.

George Gipp just happened to pass by, and joined in the game, which quickly became the talk of the neighborhood.

42

*Gipp entered Notre Dame on a baseball scholarship but was recruited to play football when coach Rockne saw him drop-kick a football nearly 70 yards.*

*The scene was reenacted by actor and future President of the United States, Ronald Reagan, in the movie 'Knute Rockne, All American.'*

*On October 4, 1940, the world premiere of 'Knute Rockne, All-American' took place in South Bend. The movie, starring actor Pat O'Brien as Rockne, was shown in the four local theaters: the Granada, Palace, Colfax, and State.*

In this shared moment of unexpected joy, Teddy understood that the true spirit of Notre Dame wasn't just in its victories or legends, but in the community and connections formed in these spontaneous, magical gatherings.

Teddy felt a deep sense of gratitude for the community that embraced him and the friendships that enriched his life.

He started to learn that Notre Dame's legacy wasn't just built on the achievements of its past but on the collective spirit of its people who came together to celebrate, to mourn, and to uplift each other.

Teddy, Snacks, and their new friends were just beginning their adventures.

As they explored South Bend together, their bonds grew stronger, and the town transformed from a mere residence into a true home, rich with camaraderie and cherished memories.

Each outing, from spirited sports games to overnight camp outs, solidified their friendships and deepened their connection to the vibrant South Bend community they now called their own.

But Teddy and Snacks were also becoming an integral part of the Notre Dame community, a welcoming and supportive environment that embraced them and prepared them for a future filled with promise and purpose.

43

# Chapter Ten

## Jimmy Comes to Visit

Summer vacation finally arrived, and Teddy couldn't wait for Jimmy to visit from Chicago.

Teddy had known his best friend, James Edward Murphy, or 'Jimmy,' since he was three years old.

They met because their mothers worked together in the tearoom at the Blackstone Hotel in Chicago, and they just happened to live one street apart.

The two friends were inseparable until Teddy moved to South Bend, a change that was also tough on Jimmy.

Jimmy was eagerly looking forward to his trip to South Bend to see his best friend, and he couldn't wait for the day to arrive.

When the day finally arrived, Teddy, Snacks, *'Pee Wee'*, *'Ned'*, and *'Lure King'* warmly welcomed Jimmy at the South Shore Station in South Bend.

Snacks was especially excited to see Jimmy.

Upon spotting his old friend, Snacks repeatedly ran in figure eights around him to show his happiness.

"Hi, Snacks!" Jimmy exclaimed. "I missed you, boy," he said as he scratched Snacks behind the ear and then shook Teddy's hand.

Jimmy fit in with the gang immediately, just like *"peanut butter and chocolate"* or *"hot butter on popcorn."*

One afternoon, the group of friends decided to have a picnic near the Studebaker plant where Teddy's dad worked.

There they played baseball, while Snacks chased butterflies and fly balls, and everyone enjoyed the warm summer day.

Teddy and Snacks also took Jimmy on a tour of the Notre Dame campus and introduced him to the school's traditions and landmarks.

Jimmy was awestruck with Notre Dame.

Everything about the campus, especially the architecture of the buildings, captivated his attention.

Jimmy, walking beside Teddy and Snacks, marveled at the history and tradition that seemed to seep from every brick, already envisioning the many new memories they would create together in this inspiring place.

As they walked around Saint Mary's Lake one afternoon, as the sun cast a golden glow on its waters, Jimmy, too, experienced a profound sense of belonging and inspiration.

This visit wasn't just an introduction to the historic university for him; it was a moment that deeply touched his heart.

"This is where I want to go to school when I get older," Jimmy told Teddy.

He returned home to Chicago a week later, and although Teddy was sad to see his best friend go home, he no longer felt as lonely as he once did.

Over the next few years, Jimmy made several trips to South Bend to see Teddy and Snacks and, of course, visit Notre Dame.

Jimmy's growing connection with Notre Dame inspired him to study hard in school, hoping that one day he might attend the university.

Teddy and Jimmy's friendship was built on shared dreams and mutual encouragement. Despite being miles apart, they exchanged letters, motivating each other to excel in school.

They often spoke about their aspirations and dreams, and in one of their letters, they made a solemn promise to attend Notre Dame together, with Snacks by their side.

They knew the journey would be tough, but they were committed to supporting each other through every challenge.

A few years later, as they neared high school graduation, they applied to Notre Dame. In their admissions essays, they wrote about their deep friendship, shared dreams, and commitment to making a positive impact on the world.

## Chapter Eleven

## The Inspiration to Teach

In the fall of '19, Teddy and Snacks found themselves immersed in a true Notre Dame adventure, thanks to 'Gipp.'

Instead of heading home after school, the two made a beeline to Cartier Field to help Coach Rockne and the Notre Dame football team at practice.

It was a privilege they had never anticipated just a few months before, but one that brought them even closer to the heart of the Notre Dame experience than they could have ever imagined.

Under the autumn sun that season, Teddy helped set up drills, fetched water, and offered moral support to the players, while Snacks kept the players entertained with his antics.

Coach Rockne welcomed Teddy and Snacks with open arms, treating them not just as helpers, but as an integral part of the team.

Their dedication and enthusiasm did not go unnoticed, earning them respect and admiration from the players and coaching staff alike.

The experience not only deepened Teddy's love for football and Notre Dame, but it also taught him valuable lessons about teamwork, perseverance, and the importance of supporting one another.

*The 1919 Notre Dame football team finished the season undefeated at 9-0, outscoring their opponents 229-47., and was named co-national champions by the National Championship Foundation and Parke H. Davis.*

Working with Coach Rockne opened Teddy's eyes to a path he knew he wanted to pursue: to become a coach and teacher.

Coach Rockne had a way of speaking that made you listen, not just hear, and taught his players about more than just football; he taught them about life.

Rock had a knack for finding a person's hidden potential and nurturing it into something extraordinary.

Rock taught Teddy that it wasn't about the victories on the field, nor the cheers from the crowds that were important, but the lessons learned in practice and off the field that prepared players for games and life.

Gipp also introduced Teddy and Snacks to other individuals on campus who would eventually become good friends, impact his life, and assist him in his journey to becoming a teacher.

One of those individuals was Father Cornelius Hagerty, who taught philosophy classes at Notre Dame and was popular with the student body.

*Father Con'* was also an outdoor enthusiast who would take Teddy, Snacks, Gipp, and other students on canoe trips on the St. Joseph River, which flowed behind the St. Mary's College campus and through the city of South Bend.

*In his autobiography, Father Hagerty recounts George Gipp having to 'swim for his life' after his canoe capsized in the St. Joe River, and later telling a near- death Father Peyton in 1938, "The blessed Mother will be as good to you as you believe." After a night of prayer and vowing to promote the rosary, Peyton miraculously recovered and devoted his life to the devotion.*

And so, with Snacks by his side, Teddy Flynn settled into his new life in South Bend, where he began his connection to the University of Notre Dame and began pursuing his dream of becoming a coach and teacher.

All thanks to a wayward football and a chance meeting with one of Notre Dame football's all-time greats, George Gipp.

# Chapter Twelve

## 'Win One for The Gipper'

"And that, Patty, is how Snacks and I got that autographed football and made my first friend in South Bend," Ted concluded.

"You knew George Gipp?" Patty asked, amazed. "George Gipp actually signed this football. My dad won't believe it," she added.

*You can see similar footballs and other historic Notre Dame football memorabilia at Augie's Locker Room in South Bend.*

"Gipp excelled in everything he did," Ted said, with a lump in his throat. "I'll always be grateful for his friendship."

Teddy only knew George Gipp for a short time, as Gipp died on December 14, 1920, from complications of strep throat and pneumonia, and just two weeks after being named Notre Dame's first *Walter Camp All-American.*

*Back then they didn't have the antibiotics that we have today, which could have saved Gipp's life.*

You might have also heard the phrase, *'Win one for the Gipper.'*

That's when Knute Rockne told the story of George Gipp's final wish for a Notre Dame team to win a big game for him one day.

During halftime of the 1928 game against Army at Yankee Stadium in New York, Rockne delivered the *'Gipper'* speech to rally Notre Dame to a 12-6 victory.

Running back Jack Chevigny, a native of Hammond, Indiana, scored the winning touchdown for Notre Dame and is reported to have said, *'that's one for the Gipper,'* as he crossed the goal line.

Here's what Knute Rockne told his team on that November day:

*"I've got to go, Rock. It's all right. I'm not afraid. Some time, Rock, when the team is up against it, when things are wrong and the breaks are beating the boys, ask them to go in there with all they've got and win just one for the Gipper. I don't know where I'll be then, Rock. But I'll know about it, and I'll be happy."*

"Gipp sure made an impact on me as a young boy," Ted said, as he wiped the tears from his eyes.

"I was devastated when he died."

"To honor his memory, I followed his advice and studied hard in school," Ted reminisced.

"I remember those late nights with my lamp burning well past midnight," he said. "I poured over textbooks and assignments, always with his words echoing in my mind."

"I was fortunate enough to be accepted into Notre Dame, an opportunity I never took for granted," Ted said. "I felt the weight of history and the responsibility to make my own mark."

Working with Coach Rockne and the football team was more than a privilege to Teddy—it was a testament to the power of perseverance and the fulfillment of his dream.

"My time at Notre Dame was about more than classes; it was about the spirit, community, and Coach Rockne's lessons in leadership and resilience," Ted said. "Those experiences laid the foundation for my teaching career."

"It helped shape me into the man I am today," he said with conviction. "A man who values hard work, giving back, and honoring those who came before us. Notre Dame wasn't just my alma mater; it forged my character and commitment to making a difference."

# Chapter Thirteen

## The Four Horsemen

Time swiftly passed for Teddy as he grew up in the vibrant surroundings of South Bend, with the iconic University of Notre Dame casting its storied shadow over his upbringing.

In 1924, Teddy, now 14 years old, served as a special assistant to Coach Rockne. To him, it was the most prestigious job on the team, nearly as important as being the head coach.

Teddy looked up at the clock as he fidgeted in his desk at school. "2:57 p.m. Only three more minutes until the bell rings," he thought.

Those final three minutes of school that Monday afternoon seemed to drag on for an eternity, but Teddy was ready to go once the bell rang.

He had planned his route carefully and knew it would only take seven and a half minutes to get to Cartier Field on the Notre Dame campus from his school.

"Coach Rockne doesn't like tardiness," he said to himself, as he quickly skirted out the door.

During football season, Teddy was the first student out of the school door on Mondays and Wednesdays, and Snacks, as usual, was there to greet him.

Snacks barked and jumped up to lick Teddy's face before the two 'double-timed' it to practice.

At practice Teddy did odd jobs for Coach Rockne and the football team. He wore a team-issued gray sweatshirt with the ND monogram on the front and even had his own whistle.

Coach Rockne even had a job for Snacks: retrieving footballs that strayed away from the practice field. Rock even said that Snacks was the best 'wide retriever' he had ever seen.

The 1924 Notre Dame football team had a good start to the season, holding a record of 2-0 after defeating Lombard in the opener and Wabash College 34-0 the previous Saturday.

The opposition had not scored a point against the Notre Dame defense in two straight games, and Coach Rockne was pleased. However, he intended to maintain this record against their upcoming opponent, Army.

Army was one of Notre Dame's toughest and biggest rivals and boasted one of the best teams in the country.

The eagerly anticipated game was set to be held at the Polo Grounds in New York City, where a huge crowd was expected, including many Notre Dame Subway Alumni.

Practice was all business that week, and Teddy and Snacks knew they had to be 'on their game' to help the team win.

That season, Notre Dame featured one of the most powerful backfields in school history.

Although each player was talented individually, it was the combined excellence of their collective efforts in the backfield that truly highlighted their greatness.

The sum was, indeed, greater than the individual parts.

These four individuals were Harry Stuhldreher, Don Miller, Elmer Layden, and Jim Crowley.

Teddy and Snacks were proud to be friends with all the players, and one of their jobs was to help warm up the arm of quarterback Harry Stuhldreher by playing catch with him.

Little did Teddy and Snacks know that the game against Army that season would become one of the most important in the history of college football.

The two worked hard to get the team ready, just as they did every week, but the team only had a few days to practice since the train for the trip to New York was scheduled to leave on that Thursday morning.

Teddy couldn't travel with the team, but he and Snacks had an important job on game days when the team was on the road.

On game days, Teddy served refreshments at the newly built Knights of Columbus Indiana Club in downtown South Bend, where people gathered for lunch and to listen to the radio broadcast of Notre Dame football games.

Teddy also helped set up the radio and speakers, while Snacks welcomed the guests to the hall and helped lead cheers with his barking.

"Hurry up everybody!" Teddy yelled. "The game is about to start."

It was going to be a tough battle that afternoon with Army, but Notre Dame was well prepared.

Notre Dame scored the game's first touchdown when *'Sleepy'* Jim Crowley crossed the goal line to make the score Notre Dame 6, Army 0.

"Atta boy, Jim," Teddy cheered, as Snacks ran around in circles and barked to celebrate the touchdown.

Crowley would score again, and the Notre Dame defense would limit Army to just one touchdown, to make the final score Notre Dame 13, Army 7.

During the game, the famous sportswriter Grantland Rice, of the *New York Herald Tribune,* was quite taken by the Notre Dame backfield's *'surgeon-like precision,'* a sentiment he shared with his sports writing colleagues.

Teddy's friend George Strickler, who served as the publicist for Coach Rockne, overheard the sportswriters discussing the Notre Dame backfield in the press box.

Now, George enjoyed going to the movies and was a big fan of the actor Rudolph Valentino, who starred in the movie *'The Four Horsemen of the Apocalypse'* a few years earlier, in 1921.

*Valentino was married in Crown Point, Indiana in 1923. From 1915 to 1940, the city was well- known as a 'marriage mill,' with many celebrities, including Ronald Reagan, choosing to get married there.*

George watched the movie with the rest of the team on Wednesday night at Washington Hall, after practice and before the trip east. Teddy and Snacks even got to watch the movie with them.

After the movie, George told Teddy and Snacks that the Notre Dame backfield was just like the *'Four Horsemen'* depicted in the movie.

"I've got an idea to help promote the team," he said, while Teddy and Snacks wished him good luck on the trip east and with his idea.

54

During the game, George mentioned to Grantland Rice that the Notre Dame backfield— Stuhldreher, Miller, Layden, and Crowley—reminded him of 'The Four Horsemen of the Apocalypse,' giving the New York Herald Tribune sportswriter an idea for his game story that has become one the most famous sports journalism leads of all-time.

The following day, his paper and others across the country published the account of the game that was played on October 18, 1924:

*"Outlined against a blue-gray October sky the Four Horsemen rode again. In dramatic lore they are known as famine, pestilence, destruction, and death. These are only aliases. Their real names are: Stuhldreher, Miller, Crowley and Layden. They formed the crest of the South Bend cyclone before which another fighting Army team was swept over the precipice at the Polo Grounds this afternoon as 55,000 spectators peered down upon the bewildering panorama spread out upon the green plain below."*

Teddy read the wire service report in the *South Bend Tribune* that Sunday morning, while lying on his living room floor. He then carefully cut out the article to add to his scrapbook, which bore '*1924*' on the cover.

Teddy looked over at his companion and stated, "Snacks, do you think Notre Dame can win the national championship this season?"

Snacks replied with an enthusiastic bark.

On Monday, following the game, Teddy couldn't wait until 3 p.m. There would be no practice that afternoon because the team's train wasn't scheduled to arrive in South Bend until 6:15 p.m. and Teddy wanted to be there to greet the team.

After school, Teddy went home and asked his mom and dad if he could go meet the train and the team after dinner. His dad said, "Let's go ask Gran and Grandad Flynn if they want to come, and we'll all welcome the team together."

Teddy and his family then drove to downtown South Bend in their Studebaker, and when they arrived at the station, there was already a huge crowd gathered to welcome the team home.

The Notre Dame Band, the oldest college marching band in the nation, was present and played the 'Victory March' non-stop.

Upon hearing the fight song, Grandma Flynn started doing an Irish jig, and Snacks happily joined in, dancing alongside her.

A few minutes later, Snacks started barking as puffs of smoke and the faint sound of the train whistle could be seen and heard coming from the east.

It was the Notre Dame team train!

The train pulled into the station and came to a hissing stop. As soon as the last gasp of steam bellowed, the band struck up the 'Victory March' one more time.

Coach Rockne was the first one off the train and gave a speech to the enthusiastic crowd.

Then members of the team were introduced by the Notre Dame student government president as they stepped off the train.

"And here they are, the 'Four Horsemen,'" the student leader announced.

Everyone in the country knew about the now-famous Notre Dame backfield from the newspaper article.

As George Strickler got off the train, he spotted Teddy. "Teddy!" he yelled. "Did you see the papers?"

George then mentioned an idea and how he needed Teddy's help after Wednesday's practice. He whispered the idea into Teddy's ear.

When Teddy heard the idea, he grinned like the Cheshire Cat in "Alice in Wonderland."

Now, as I mentioned, George Strickler was Rockne's publicist, and he had the idea to make the name *'Four Horsemen'* a household name.

"Teddy, we need to get four horses so we can put the players on them for a photograph," said George. "I'll find a photographer if you can find out where we can get the horses," said George.

Teddy knew exactly where he could find the horses; Mr. Anderson from the Knights of Columbus also worked at the livery stable in downtown South Bend.

So, after practice on that Wednesday, George had his photographer friend show up, while Teddy and Snacks paraded over to Cartier Field with Mr. Anderson leading four plow horses from the livery stable.

The hardest part of the plan was getting the *'Four Horsemen'* onto the horses. A few of them had never even been close to a horse, and if you look closely at the photo, you might even see a look of fright on their faces.

The players were eventually coaxed into mounting the horses as the photographer snapped the iconic photo that you've probably seen many times, but now you know the story behind the photograph.

George thanked Teddy and Snacks for their help and then asked, "Do you know where I can get seven mules? We can't let the backfield get all the notoriety," he laughed.

The photo was picked up by the wire services and sent to newspapers all over the country, putting faces to the name *'Four Horsemen'* and immortalizing them into gridiron history.

Notre Dame finished the season undefeated, with a record of 10-0, which included a victory over Stanford in the 1925 Rose Bowl and was awarded the national championship for 1924.

Teddy and Snacks were part of that team, and they captured every moment in their scrapbook.

Teddy's friend, George Strickler, would go on to a career in journalism and became the sports editor of the *Chicago Tribune*, while the quartet of Stuhldreher, Miller, Layden, and Crowley, the *'Four Horsemen'*, were immortalized in college football lore.

Grantland Rice's prose emerged as some of the most iconic in the history of sports journalism, immortalizing the legendary *'Four Horsemen of Notre Dame.'* Yet, what often goes unnoticed is the modest, yet impactful role that Teddy and Snacks played in shaping what became one of Notre Dame's greatest football seasons.

While the spotlight was on the quartet of Miller, Stuhldreher, Crowley, and Layden, it was the quiet dedication and support of individuals like Teddy and Snacks that laid the groundwork for their success.

From organizing practices to ensuring the team was mentally and physically prepared, their contributions, though behind the scenes, were vital.

Their efforts, combined with the brilliance of the *'Four Horsemen,'* turned that season into a hallmark of excellence, forever etched in the annals of college football history.

## Chapter Fourteen

## A Dark Shadow Over Campus

The day had started like any other, with the promise of spring breathing life into South Bend. *'Ted,'* as he was now known, was a 21-year-old junior at Notre Dame.

He had woken up that morning to the sound of birds chirping and the sight of sunlight streaming through his dorm room window at Sorin Hall.

Snacks, ever the early riser, was already wagging his tail at the edge of the bed, eager for the start of another day's adventures.

As the two set out for their morning walk to class, the air was filled with the kind of hope that only comes with the changing of seasons.

Usually, when Ted tossed a ball to Snacks, he chased after it with boundless energy. But that morning, despite the bright and sunny weather, something suddenly didn't seem or feel right.

Now, dogs have a special sixth sense—you know, that special 'gut feeling' you get when something doesn't feel right. Snacks was no different and had the extraordinary gift of knowing how to deal with people and situations.

Snacks suddenly began whimpering, prompting a concerned Ted to ask, "What's wrong, boy?"

Snacks continued to whimper and didn't want Ted to leave him by going to class and kept grabbing for his hand.

"It'll be OK, boy, I'm here," Ted reassured him. "It'll be OK."

But it wouldn't be OK, and things would never be the same again at Notre Dame.

The tranquility of that Tuesday morning on March 31, 1931, was shattered by the news that spread through the campus like wildfire.

You know, the type of news that makes your heart sink and leaves you speechless.

Coach Knute Rockne, the heart and soul of Notre Dame Football, had perished in a plane crash in the Kansas Flint Hills.

Flight 599, a Fokker F-10 owned by Transcontinental and Western Air, crashed near Bazaar, Kansas, shortly after taking off from the Kansas City Municipal Airport in Kansas City, Missouri, killing everyone on board.

Coach Rockne was on his way to Los Angeles to be a consultant on the production of a movie that was being produced titled, 'The Spirit of Notre Dame' starring Lew Ayres.

The shocking news hit Ted and his classmates like a freight train, leaving them in a state of disbelief.

60

Coach Rockne wasn't just a local hero; he was a national icon, a symbol of perseverance, and the architect of the Fighting Irish's success. But more importantly, he was their hero.

Rock had been a mentor, a father figure, and a beacon of integrity to many students at Notre Dame. Especially to Ted and Snacks.

As the world mourned, Ted found himself reflecting on the lessons he had learned from Coach Rockne about teamwork, perseverance, and the pursuit of excellence, which inspired him and helped shape him into the person he was becoming.

The news of the plane crash cast a dark shadow over campus and South Bend, but in its wake, it also unified the community.

Ted realized that the spirit of Coach Rockne would live on, not just in the storied halls of Notre Dame, but in the hearts of those he had touched.

He was starting to understand that life, much like the game of football, must go on. It was up to everyone at Notre Dame to carry forward Rockne's legacy, striving for greatness while facing adversity with courage and grace.

On the day before Easter in 1931, at 3 p.m. Central Time, 5,000 mourners gathered at Sacred Heart Parish as CBS Radio sent its feed to its 79 affiliates across the country, with WGN-AM, Chicago, and WSBT-AM, South Bend also broadcasting the funeral service of Knute Rockne.

*Rockne's funeral mass was the first to be internationally broadcast on radio and was held at the same place where Professor Jerome Green sent the first wireless radio transmission on the North American continent.*

More than 150 former players, teammates, coaching colleagues, and friends of Coach Rockne were listed as honorary pallbearers.

Ted and Snacks were among those listed, and they sat next to New York Mayor Jimmy Walker, a friend of Rock's, at the funeral Mass.

Rev. Charles L. O'Donnell, then president of Notre Dame, gave Rockne's eulogy in which he said:

*"In this holy week of Christ's passion and death, there has occurred a tragic event which accounts for our presence here today. Knute Rockne is dead. And who was he?*

*Ask the president of the United States, who dispatched a personal message of tribute to his memory and comfort to his bereaved family.*

*Ask the king of Norway, who sends a special delegation as his personal representatives to this solemn service.*

*Ask the several state legislatures, now sitting, that have passed resolutions of sympathy and condolence.*

*Ask the university senates, the civic bodies, and societies without number; ask the bishops, the clergy, the religious orders, that have sent assurances of sympathy and prayers.*

*Ask the thousands of newspapermen, whose labor of love in his memory has stirred a reading public of 125 million Americans. Ask men and women from every walk of life; ask the children, the boys of America, ask any and all of these, who was this man whose death has struck nations with dismay and has everywhere bowed heads in grief?*

*Of necessity, we are few in number in this hallowed place, though thousands are without the doors. But we represent millions of men and women like ourselves who are here in spirit, in the very spirit of these solemn services, and listening all over America to these holy rites."*

Coach Rockne was buried at Highland Cemetery in South Bend, just a few miles from campus. Six of his players from the previous year - Marty Brill, Tom Yarr, Frank Carideo, Marchy Schwartz, Tom Conley, and Larry Mullins - carried him to his final resting place.

*In April 2024, the casket of the legendary football coach was exhumed from Highland Cemetery in South Bend and reburied at the University of Notre Dame, along with the graves of his wife, son, and grandson.*

In 13 seasons at Notre Dame, Rockne's record included 105 wins, 12 losses, and five ties, along with three national championships.

His .881 winning percentage is the highest in major college football history, and his record included five undefeated seasons, and six others where his team lost only one game.

The loss of Coach Rockne was a turning point for Ted, a moment that taught him about the fragility of life and the strength of legacy.

As Notre Dame slowly began to heal, Ted and Snacks continued their daily routines, each day taking a little step forward in the long process of moving on, and always carrying with them the spirit of a coach who had taught them about more than just football.

It just seemed a little harder.

When Ted threw a ball to Snacks, he still chased after it, but without the boundless energy and passion that he had just a few days before.

Ted was concerned about his friend as he, too, had a *'gut feeling'* that something was wrong.

He watched Snacks more closely over the next few days, noticing the way he moved a bit slower, how he seemed to tire more easily, and how his once-joyful barks had turned into quiet whimpers.

Ted decided to take Snacks to the local vet, hoping to find out what was troubling his faithful companion and to bring back the lively spirit that had always been a hallmark of their adventures together.

# Chapter Fifteen

## Snacks

"Mr. Flynn," Patty said. "Is that Snacks with you in the picture?

"Yep," Ted said, as his voice began to quiver.

"Snacks was the best dog a boy could ever have asked for, and he sure meant a lot to me," he added.

"We got him when I was seven years old," Ted said. "My dad's friend's dog had a litter of puppies, and I remember the day we went to see them."

As Teddy was watching the puppies, they were all over the place, tumbling and playing. Then, this one tiny pup, a bit nosier and bolder than the others, came waddling over to him and gave his hand a little nuzzle.

Right then and there, it was like something clicked. Total love at first sight.

The precocious pup, with its soft fur and bright, engaging eyes, seemed to choose Teddy, and without hesitation, he knew this was the puppy he wanted.

"Can we keep him, Dad?" Teddy asked. "Please?"

Seeing the two of them together, Teddy's dad couldn't say no, and Snacks became part of the Flynn family.

Teddy named him 'Snacks' because the little character kept trying to get at the treats he had brought for the puppies.

Now, Snacks was no ordinary dog. He became a special friend to everyone at Notre Dame and had the uncanny ability to sense when someone was feeling down and was always there to cheer them up.

"I can still see him wagging his tail and walking around campus like he was a sophomore," Ted fondly recalled.

"He loved being around students, going to the Grotto, and cheering on Notre Dame," Ted said, as tears rolled down his cheeks.

"Everyone loved him, and he even lived with me in the dorm when I went to school," he added.

Snacks passed away just a month after Coach Rockne's fatal plane crash, and merely a few days before graduation ceremonies.

"I found him curled up on my monogram blanket in my dorm room after class one day that spring during my junior year," Ted said, with tears in his eyes.

"I guess after losing Rock, and with the campus being so sad, it just broke his little heart," Ted recounted.

"We buried him near Holy Cross Cemetery on campus the next day," he added tearfully.

Jimmy and many other friends were there to say goodbye to Snacks.

"Snacks sure was a good friend, and you were lucky to have him," Patty said, as she was nearly in tears. "He was quite the character," she added.

"He sure was, Patty" Ted said. "He was tops, and I still miss him."

There was even a tribute to Snack's in the 1932 Dome Yearbook:

*"In loving memory of 'Snacks,' whose unwavering loyalty and joyful spirit brought endless laughter and comfort to our hallowed halls, forever reminding us of the power of friendship and the irreplaceable bond between humans and their four-legged companions."*

*-1932 Dome Staff*

# Chapter Sixteen

## Portage, Indiana

Upon graduating from Notre Dame, Ted began a journey that took him back to the classroom— this time, not as a student, but as a high school teacher.

With a passion for education ignited during his time working with Coach Rockne and learning from Father Hagerty, Ted sought to share his knowledge and enthusiasm with the next generation.

After completing his student teaching, Ted was ready to take on a more permanent role in education, and it wasn't long before he learned of an opportunity that seemed tailor-made for him at Portage High School in the town which would become Portage, Indiana.

Drawn to the school's commitment to excellence and its growing community, Ted knew this was where he wanted to be, in a town close to Chicago and South Bend.

*Before Portage became a town, it consisted of three communities: McCool, Crisman, and Garyton. In 1959, Portage was incorporated as a town, and in 1967 it became a city and was one of the fastest growing communities in the country. Today, Portage is the largest city in Porter County, and the third largest in Northwest Indiana with a population in 2020 of 37,926 residents.*

Ted applied for the teaching position at Portage High School, eager to bring his own ideas and energy to the classroom and waited anxiously for a response.

He received a letter in the mail that contained details for an on-site interview, marking the next step in his journey to securing the job.

During his interview, he presented letters of reference, including a letter that Rock wrote to him in his junior year, a month before he died.

Here's what that letter said:

*Dear Teddy,*

*I've heard the wonderful news about your acceptance to become a student teacher, and I couldn't be prouder.*

*Your journey, marked by perseverance and a relentless drive to overcome challenges, has always inspired those around you.*

*Now, as you stand on the brink of shaping young minds, I have no doubt that you will bring the same resilience, passion, and leadership to the classroom that you bring to the practice field as student manager.*

*Remember, Teddy, teaching is much like coaching. It's about guiding, inspiring, and bringing out the best in each individual.*

*Your unique story, your struggles, and triumphs, are powerful lessons in themselves. Share them.*

*Let your students see the strength in vulnerability, the value in hard work, and the importance of never giving up.*

*I look forward to hearing about your successes, in and out of the classroom.*

*You've always been a fighter, a leader, and now, you want to be a teacher. And what a fine one you will be.*

*With all my support and best wishes,*

*Rock*
*February 15, 1931*

Two days after his interview, Ted received a phone call asking him if he would like to become part of the Portage High School faculty.

His dedication to his students was evident from the start, as he didn't just teach; he inspired.

Whether it was through innovative teaching methods, personalized attention to students' needs, or his ability to connect real-world experiences to classroom lessons, Ted quickly became a favorite among students and colleagues alike.

At Portage High School, he wasn't just teaching subjects; he was nurturing young minds and shaping their futures, leaving a lasting impact on the community he grew to love.

After settling into his role, Ted's life took another joyful turn when he met his future wife, Julia, a fellow educator with whom he shared a passion for making a difference.

Julia Albright was also a new teacher at Portage and started the same year as Ted, teaching home economics. She was a local girl who graduated from nearby Jackson Township High School.

*Jackson Township High School was consolidated into the Duneland School Corporation with students now attending Chesterton High School. The school also graduated Portage Athletic Trainer Robert "Doc" Kerns, one of the first athletic trainers in Indiana.*

Ted and Julia were married in a heartfelt ceremony at Sacred Heart Parish on the Note Dame campus. They exchanged their vows before family and friends, with Father Hagerty officiating the union and Jimmy serving as *"best man."*

As they built their life together in Portage, Ted and Julia welcomed three children: Mary, a St. Mary's College graduate who followed in her parents' footsteps to become a teacher; George, a United States Naval Academy graduate who rose to the rank of colonel in the United States Marine Corps; and Teddy Jr., a student manager under Coach Ara Parseghian, who graduated from Notre Dame and became an advertising executive in Chicago.

The Flynn children were raised in a nurturing environment filled with love, learning, laughter, and, of course, Notre Dame football.

"They even had a dog, the spitting image of Snacks, whom they named *Freckles*.'"

The Flynns were deeply engaged in the Portage community and were active parishioners at St. Francis Xavier in East Gary, Indiana. Their devotion continued to Nativity of Our Savior after the new Catholic church was built in Portage during the 1960s.

*East Gary was originally known as Lake Station, platted in 1852 along the Michigan Central Railroad, and served as an important shipping center for agricultural products. The town became part of the new suburb of East Gary in 1908. City boosters hoped to attract executives from Gary, but workers came instead. In 1977, East Gary was renamed Lake Station.*

Ted's unwavering commitment to his students was only paralleled by his dedication to his family, creating a legacy of education and kindness that resonated both within the classroom and at home.

Evenings often found Ted at the kitchen table, immersed in grading papers or preparing lesson plans, surrounded by his children who eagerly observed and learned from their father's dedication.

He transformed learning into a family affair, fostering spirited discussions on history, science, and literature during family dinners. Ted and Julia cultivated a home environment that cherished curiosity and lifelong learning.

Ted's dedication extended far beyond academics; he was known throughout the community for his volunteer work, constantly seeking ways to give back and uplift those around him.

His influence left an indelible mark not only on his students but also on his family, instilling a deep love for knowledge and a spirit of compassion that resonated through every life he touched.

# Chapter Seventeen

## Loyal Sons and Daughters

"I can't believe you actually knew George Gipp, Knute Rockne, and the Four Horsemen," Patty said. "Thank you so much for sharing your story."

"You're welcome," said Ted, as he cleared his throat and got up from the desk.

"Well, I'd better get back to grading," he said, while walking back towards the stack of term papers. "And you'd better start to think about where you're going to apply to college next year," he added.

"I've already decided where I want to go to school, Mr. Flynn," said Patty.

"I know," Ted said with pride. "Superintendent Burton told me you're interested in attending Notre Dame. Do you know what you'd like to study?"

"I do," said Patty. "Shelley Aylesworth and I are both applying to the architecture program. It's been our dream to go to school there since they started accepting women last fall."

*The first class of female undergraduate students appeared at Notre Dame in the fall of 1972, the same year that Title IX became law to prohibit discrimination. Former Indiana Senator Birch Bayh played an instrumental role in its passage and is considered the 'Father of Title IX.'*

*Today, women comprise 49% of the students admitted to Notre Dame.*

*In recent years, the school's fight song, the 'Notre Dame Victory March,' has been updated to acknowledge the contributions of women to the school, and it now features the lyrics 'While her loyal sons and daughters march on to victory. Additionally, in 2023, the school introduced its first female Leprechaun mascot.*

"Always follow and believe in your dreams," Ted said to Patty. "It worked for me, and it will work for you, too," he added.

He then said, "Patty, Notre Dame has a world class architecture program, and it's ranked in the top 10% of all schools in the country. Let me know if I can help you and Shelley with your applications."

"That is so kind of you, Mr. Flynn. But how do you know so much about the architecture program?" Patty questioned.

"Oh, I have my ways," laughed Ted.

"I bet you do," Patty said with a laugh. "Say, whatever happened to your friend, Jimmy?"

"Jim? He's still my best friend," Ted said, in an upbeat voice.

"We roomed together at Notre Dame, and he still lives in our old neighborhood in Chicago, where he's an architect."

"An architect?" said Patty, in a surprised voice. "I can't believe it."

"Yep, he's one of the best in the world," Ted said, "and he'll be happy to know that you and Shelley are interested in studying architecture at Notre Dame."

*The University of Notre Dame was the first Catholic university in America to offer a degree in architecture, beginning in 1898, and continues to offer undergraduate and post-graduate architecture programs.*

"What are your plans now, Mr. Flynn?" asked Patty.

"Well, I'm going to get these papers graded, and then turn on the radio to listen to the Cubs game," Ted said.

*Despite growing up on the South Side and being a lifelong Chicago White Sox fan, Ted became a Chicago Cubs fan through his friendship with Jack Quinlan, whom he met through Notre Dame Athletic Director Moose Krause.*

72

*Unfortunately, Quinlan, the talented radio announcer and Notre Dame graduate, was killed in an automobile crash while at Cubs spring training camp in Arizona in 1965.*

Julia and I are planning a trip to Ireland this September to visit my relatives and to root for Mayo in the *GAA Football All-Ireland*. Until then, I'm going to volunteer at Indiana Dunes State Park," Ted said.

*Cork defeated Galway 3-17 to 2-13 to win the 1973 GAA All-Ireland Senior Football Championship. Mayo has not won a title since 1951. Some say this is due to the 'Mayo Curse.'*

He also added, "Jim and I are also planning to take the old *"Vomit Comet"* to a few Notre Dame games this fall."

We're looking forward to seeing our Sorin Hall dorm mates— Ron, Pat, and George," Ted said.

"What do they do," asked Patty.

"George has been an usher at Notre Dame Stadium since 1935," Ted said.

He then added, "Ron lives in northern Illinois and owns a construction company, while Pat resides in Pittsburgh and works as an accountant for U.S. Steel.

My father, who started ushering at Cartier Field, got George involved as an usher after he hired him as an engineer at the Studebaker plant."

*For many years, many of Notre Dame Stadium's ushers were local men who worked at the Studebaker and Bendix plants. Today, nearly 800 ushers from around the United States travel to South Bend to work on game days. These unsung ambassadors greet each fan with their traditional 'Welcome to Notre Dame.'*

Ted then said with a smile, "And Tom Reynolds might even stop by the Notre Dame Club of Northwest Indiana tailgate for the USC game in October."

"Wow, that sure sounds like a lot of fun," Patty said, "I hope Shelley and I get accepted into Notre Dame next year."

"Me too," Ted said. "I'll call Jim tonight and I'll also get you information on the Notre Dame Club of Northwest Indiana scholarship program."

*Approximately 150 Notre Dame clubs offer scholarships to students from their respective geographic areas. All applicants for financial aid are considered for these club scholarships.*

"Well, I'd better get going, Mr. Prescott, Coach Klein, and Coach Goodnight also need my help today," said Patty.

"Tell Lane (Prescott) he needs all the help he can get," Ted laughed. "He's a Valparaiso University grad you know."

He then added, "I'm just foolin' with you." Valpo's a great school and a couple of my boys played basketball for the Crusaders."

*Portage's Bruce Linder during the 1969-1970 basketball season at Valparaiso University set the single season record for points (725), and points per game (27.8 ppg), while Chris Lacjin played for the Crusaders (Valpo changed its name to 'Beacons' in 2021) from 1971-1974.*

*Chris Lacjin was recruited by Ara Parseghian, who visited the Portage locker room to meet him after he helped the Indians defeat seventh-ranked South Bend Adams 78-77 in overtime in the morning game of the 1971 South Bend Basketball Regional, to play football. The recruitment decision came down between Chris and Valparaiso's John Roscoe, who ultimately got the call.*

Ted then picked up the football George Gipp had signed and, with a grin, said to her, "You know, Patty, I have a feeling the '73 football season is going to be a special one for the Fighting Irish."

*The 1973 Notre Dame Fighting Irish football team, coached by Ara Parseghian, ended the season undefeated with 11 wins and no losses, and defeated Alabama 24-23 in the Sugar Bowl to clinch the national championship.*

# *Epilogue*

As the autumn leaves paint the University of Notre Dame campus in hues of gold and rust each fall, the story of Teddy Flynn and his loyal dog Snacks draws to a close.

Each day the sun continues to dip lower in the sky, casting its long shadows across these hallowed grounds where they had once roamed, dreamed, and grown.

Years have passed since Teddy, Snacks, and the Gipper walked the grounds of Notre Dame, but their legacy remains as vibrant as ever.

Alumni and new students alike whisper their names with reverence, inspired by their tales of courage, camaraderie, and conviction.

This book is more than just a story; it is a symbol of the Notre Dame spirit—a beacon for those navigating the complexities of growing up and holding fast to their dreams.

Teddy's journey from a wide-eyed boy to a man shaped by the values of Notre Dame echoes in the corridors of our hearts and of those who followed in his footsteps.

As we close this chapter, let us take with us the lessons of *Teddy and the Gipper,* and remember the importance of friendship, the pursuit of excellence, and the unyielding spirit of the *Fighting Irish* that binds us all.

For in every leaf that falls on this storied campus, in every chill wind that whispers through its trees, Teddy, Snacks, and the Gipper are there to remind us that we are never alone in our quest to make the world a better place.

Thank you for joining us on this unforgettable journey. May this story inspire you to cherish your friendships, pursue your dreams, and always, always fight the good fight.

*Len Clark, Ph.D.*

# About the Author

## Len Clark, Ph.D.

Len Clark, Ph.D. earned a graduate degree in *Communication Arts* from the University of Notre Dame and specializes in covering Notre Dame athletics using emerging media technologies. He has also served as an instructor in the university's *Gallivan Journalism Program.*

Dr. Clark has been recognized as the *'Indiana Sportscaster of the Year'* by the National Sports Media Association, from which he also received the association's national *'Powerade Award'* for his audio feature on the Notre Dame-USC football rivalry.

In 1996, Indiana Governor Evan Bayh recognized the Portage, Indiana, native and 1982 graduate of Portage High School, as a *'Sagamore of the Wabash'* in recognition of his innovative contributions to broadcasting and service to the state of Indiana.

## Jared Basker

Jared Basker is an award-winning artist hailing from South Bend, who grew up a mere stone's throw north of Notre Dame. His remarkable talent was recognized in 2014 when he received the esteemed *'Hoosier Art Patron'* Award.

Artistry runs deep in Basker's lineage, most notably through his great uncle, Edward J. Basker, a celebrated watercolor artist with significant ties to the university during the 1960s.

Drawing inspiration from Edward's legacy, Jared is renowned for his whimsical painting style that consistently captivates audiences.

If you would like to contact him about his art, the best way is through his social media pages on Facebook and Instagram under *'Jared Basker Art.'*